Desert Wildlife

Animals & Mammals

Billy Grinslott – Kinsey Marie Books

ISBN - 9781968228729

Death Valley mice, including species like the cactus mouse and desert pocket mouse, are specialized rodents adapted to extreme dry environments. They mostly feed on seeds and vegetation, and rarely need to drink standing water, obtaining moisture from their food. They possess large ears for cooling and can go into a state of torpor (lowered metabolism) to survive food and water shortages. They are primarily nocturnal and stay in burrows during the day to avoid extreme heat. They are found across various desert habitats, from valley floors to mountain shrublands.

Shrews are small with long, flexible snouts, and possess a good sense of smell and hearing to make up for poor eyesight. Desert shrews are tiny, and highly adapted nocturnal insectivores. They survive extreme heat and arid conditions by living in packrat nests. They have incredibly fast metabolisms and must eat up to their body weight daily. They obtain moisture from prey like scorpions, beetles, and spiders that they eat. Desert shrews are immune to scorpion stings. Not only are they immune to scorpion stings, but they also use a form of venom to paralyze their prey.

There are several types of woodrats. Desert woodrats are nocturnal, 9-15-inch-long rodents known as packrats. They collect sticks, cactus joints, rocks, and shiny objects to build large dens (middens) at the base of shrubs or in rock crevices. Their dens are cemented together by amberat, a substance formed from dried, crystallized urine. Their dens are often fortified with cactus spines to protect against predators like snakes and owls. They eat succulent plants, such as cactus, to obtain water, rather than drinking directly.

The Desert Kangaroo Rat got its name because it hops on two legs like a kangaroo. The kangaroo rat is perfectly adapted to life in the desert. They can survive without drinking any water, getting needed moisture from their seed diet. They have excellent hearing and can detect the sound of a flying owl approaching. Kangaroo rats have long tails and large hind feet. Their eyes are large, and their ears are small.

The Panamint chipmunk is a small, diurnal, and territorial rodent regularly occurring in rocky, pinyon-juniper woodlands in desert mountains. Primarily ground-dwelling, they are omnivores that eat seeds, fruits, insects, and vegetation, and they are known to store food to survive the winter. They have a total length of about 8-9 inches, with reddish-brown sides, gray flanks, and distinct white/dark stripes on their back and face.

White Tailed Antelope Squirrel looks a lot like a chipmunk. They also have pouches inside their mouth to carry food. The difference is they are omnivorous. Meaning, they feed on foliage, seeds, insects, lizards and rodents. Chipmunks typically don't eat meat, but the Antelope Squirrel will eat lizards and rodents. They also live in dryer climates like, deserts and foothills.

Harris's antelope squirrels are small, diurnal rodent's native to the Sonoran Desert in Arizona, New Mexico, and Mexico. Weighing 4–5 ounces, they are adapted to extreme heat, using "heat dumping" (lying flat in shade) and holding their tails over their bodies for shade. Found in desert scrub, these squirrels dig underground burrows, often beneath shrubs like creosote or mesquite. They are solitary and do not hibernate, remaining active throughout the year.

Round-tailed ground squirrels live in flat, sandy, hot desert areas. They are diurnal, often avoiding the hottest part of the day by retreating to burrows. These rodents weigh about 4.4 ounces and are roughly 8 to 11 inches in length, with about half of that being their tail. They are omnivores, eating green vegetation, seeds, and insects. They often obtain necessary moisture from their food. They use a single sharp, high-pitched whistle to warn other members of the colony about predators, such as snakes, coyotes, and hawks.

Ground squirrels live in burrows which they dig with their sharp claws and muscular legs. Unlike other squirrels they have adapted to living in treeless areas. They will climb trees if there is any in the area. Ground squirrels are one of the largest squirrel species. They grow up to a length of around 17 to 21 inches. Squirrels are important plant dispersers. They gather seeds and nuts and bury them in the dirt, which grows new plants.

The rock squirrel is a large, mottled gray-brown ground squirrel native to the southwestern U.S. Renowned as hardy survivors, they live in rocky, arid habitats, can go 100 days without water, and use their bushy tails for balance while climbing trees. They are social, omnivorous, and often do not hibernate in warmer climates. They are the largest North American ground squirrel, reaching 17–21 inches in length. They are social, living in colonies with complex, deep burrows hidden beneath rocks. They use high-pitched whistles to warn of predators and are known to confront snakes by fluffing their tails and throwing dirt.

Pocket gophers are burrowing rodents and are known for their digging activities and unique adaptations for underground life. They have very sharp claws for digging. They create complex underground tunnel systems. Their fur-lined cheek pouches, or pockets, are used to store and transport food, like roots, tubers, and grasses, back to their burrows. They can turn their cheek pouches inside out for grooming purposes. Their tails are highly sensitive and act as feelers to help them navigate the dark tunnels, even when backing up.

There are many types of rabbits in the wild, the most common is the cottontail rabbit. Cottontails are adapted and live in various habitats from grasslands to deserts. Rabbits are cute, friendly, and fun to watch. Many people have rabbits for pets. They have soft fluffy fur. They are called cottontails because they have a white fluffy tail that looks like a cotton ball. Cottontail rabbits are herbivores, they eat grasses, vegetables, and fruit in summer, and woody plants/bark in winter.

The antelope jackrabbit is a large, 9-pound desert hare found in the southwestern US, characterized by exceptionally long ears and white, flash-colored sides. They are herbivores, eating cacti, grasses, and mesquite, and can run up to 45 miles per hour. They are highly adapted to arid environments, getting moisture from plants. Their long ears act like radiators, with extensive blood vessels that expand to release heat in hot, dry environments.

The black tailed jackrabbits most identifying feature is its huge ears. The ears along with the tail are tipped with black fur. Black-tailed jackrabbits are not actually rabbits but are hares. Hares are born with fur and are larger than rabbits. They usually have longer hind legs and ears. These speedy animals can reach speeds of 40 miles an hour. They have powerful hind legs and can jump 10 feet in one jump.

Badgers have elongated heads, small ears, and black and white faces. Badgers live underground with other family members. Badgers are very social and live in groups. A badger den or sett can be centuries old and are used by many generations of badgers. Badgers are very territorial, it's best not to bother them is you see one. A group of badgers is called a cete, though they are often called clans. Badgers are largely nocturnal but reduce their activity during periods of cold weather.

Spotted skunks are listed as a protected species. They are smaller than striped skunks and have a slenderer body. Unlike striped skunks, spotted skunks are excellent climbers and can scale trees and fences. When threatened, they stand on their front legs, turn their heads, and walk towards the predator, spraying their defensive spray. Before spraying, they also stamp their front feet on the ground to warn predators. They are primarily active at night and are known for being secretive. They are omnivores, eating insects, small mammals (like mice), fruits, and birds' eggs.

Opossums or possums have strong tails and can hang from trees. One trick that a possum has, is when it feels danger is it will play dead. It will lay there and not move. Possums have white to gray face hair. Possums like to eat wood ticks. They are also immune to snakebites. Opossums are susceptible to frostbite because their hands and tails are not protected by fur. Opossums are marsupials, which means they have pouches for their young, like kangaroos and koalas.

Spotted skunks are listed as a protected species. They are smaller than striped skunks and have a slenderer body. Unlike striped skunks, spotted skunks are excellent climbers and can scale trees and fences. When threatened, they stand on their front legs, turn their heads, and walk towards the predator, spraying their defensive spray. Before spraying, they also stamp their front feet on the ground to warn predators. They are primarily active at night and are known for being secretive. They are omnivores, eating insects, small mammals (like mice), fruits, and birds' eggs.

Opossums or possums have strong tails and can hang from trees. One trick that a possum has, is when it feels danger is it will play dead. It will lay there and not move. Possums have white to gray face hair. Possums like to eat wood ticks. They are also immune to snakebites. Opossums are susceptible to frostbite because their hands and tails are not protected by fur. Opossums are marsupials, which means they have pouches for their young, like kangaroos and koalas.

Ringtails look like a racoon. They have stripes on their tails, but their face more resembles a cat. They are a member of the racoon family. Ringtails can be found in some parts of North America. Ringtails are excellent climbers capable of ascending vertical walls, trees, rocky cliffs and even cactus. They are mostly nocturnal. Ringtails are agile climbers and leapers, with hind legs that can rotate 180 degrees. Their long tails help with balance. Ringtails have anal glands that produce a foul-smelling secretion.

Coatis are a member of the raccoon family. They are found in Arizona. They are primarily found in the Sonoran and Chihuahuan deserts, including areas like the Superstition Mountains and Huachuca Mountains. Coatis have a long, pig-like snout that is flexible and used for foraging for food. They have strong arms and forelimbs, along with powerful claws, for digging and foraging. Their ankles are double-jointed, allowing them to rotate their feet over 180 degrees for descending trees headfirst. Coatis are omnivores, feeding on a variety of fruits, insects, small vertebrates, and other foods.

Marmots can't see very far. They are most active during the day because of their poor eyesight. They like to come out of their dens in the morning and afternoon. Marmots have rough fur, small ears, and short tails. Their strong feet and claws are built for digging holes in the dirt. They are nicknamed the whistle pig, for the high-pitched chirp they make to warn other group members of potential Danger. Their size varies, with adults reaching 28 inches in length and weighing up to 24 pounds. They have thick fur, short legs, and large, continuously growing teeth.

Wild black-footed ferrets are North America's only native ferret, considered highly endangered with roughly 400 left in the wild. They spend about 90% of their time underground. They are nocturnal, emerging at night to hunt. Ferrets have a strip of dark fur across their eyes that makes them look like they are wearing a mask. The black-footed ferret is the only ferret that is native to America. Black-footed ferrets were thought to be extinct twice. Black-footed ferrets are playful. Black-footed ferrets are agile climbers. Black-footed ferrets have been reintroduced to many states.

A collection of prairie dog coteries is called a prairie dog town. Prairie dog towns can cover hundreds of acres and consist of thousands of prairie dogs. Their vocabulary is more advanced than any other animal language. They got their name because they live on the prairies and their warning calls which sound like dog barks. They build mounds around their den to keep water out. Prairie dogs are small burrowing mammals that are related to squirrels. They eat grasses, roots, and seeds. A Jump-yip display is a signature behavior where a prairie dog stands on its hind legs and throws its arms out, likely to check if others are alert.

The Kit or swift foxes are native to much of the western United States and northern Mexico. Kit foxes are the smallest foxes in North America, weighing only about five pounds.. Despite their slender size, they have large ears to help aid their hearing and to dissipate heat. Kit foxes are mainly active at night and resting in their dens during the day. kit foxes can survive without fresh water, by getting all their fluids from their food.

The gray fox can be identified by its coat color which is silver-gray on its back and face, reddish on its legs and chest and white on its throat, mid-belly, and the insides of it legs. The Gray fox prefers to live in rocky canyons and ridges but can also be found in wooded areas and open fields. The gray fox is the only member of the dog family that will climb trees. They have strong, hooked claws that enable them to climb trees, which is abnormal for a dog species.

The coyote is bigger than a fox weighing between 20 and 45 pounds. Eastern coyotes are part wolf. Coyotes are great for pest control. They like to eat mice and rats. They can adapt and live almost anywhere, even in the city. Coyotes are very smart and have been observed learning and following traffic signals in some cities. They have a yip type of call when they communicate with each other. Coyotes are found in all the United States, except Hawaii.

Mexican gray wolves are the smallest subspecies of gray wolf, reaching a height of 25-32 inches and weighing between 50 and 85 pounds, and are also the rarest in North America. Mexican gray wolves are uniquely adapted to the arid environments of the southwestern U.S. and northern Mexico. They live in packs led by an alpha pair, with a complex hierarchy that helps the pack function as a unit. They communicate through howling, scent marking, and body language, including tail wagging, yipping, and growling.

Bobcats are named for their short, bobbed tails with white tips. They have similar markings to lynxes but are much smaller. Bobcats live in a variety of habitats. Bobcats are skilled at leaping and can run up to 30 miles per hour.

Ocelot cats are rare, endangered, medium-sized wild cats in the USA, with fewer than 100 individuals surviving in the South Texas brushlands. They are about twice the size of a house cat. No two ocelots have the same markings on their fur. They have their own unique markings. They also have ringed bars along the full length of their tails. Ocelots are most active under the cover of darkness. They are primarily nocturnal, hunting small mammals, rodents, reptiles, and birds.

The cougar has several different names, it's also known as the puma or mountain lion. They are the fourth largest cat in the world. The cougar has the largest range of any wild cat in the North America. A cougar can jump upward 18 feet from a sitting position. They can leap up to 30 feet horizontally. Cougars cannot roar like a lion, but they can make calls that sounds like a human scream. They are the largest cats in North America, weighing up to 225 pounds and measuring 6 feet in length.

Aoudad (Barbary sheep) are highly adaptable, non-native game animals introduced to the US from North Africa in the 1950s. As an invasive species, they thrive in arid, rocky terrain, competing with native desert bighorn sheep. They are known for their extreme climbing ability, rapid reproduction, and large curved horns. They occupy the same rugged, dry, rocky habitats as native bighorn sheep. They are mostly active at dawn and dusk. Males can weigh up to 320 pounds, with both sexes featuring long, shaggy hair on their throats and chest (often called "chaps"). Their horns can reach over 30 inches in length.

Javelinas, or collared peccaries, are native, social mammals common in Arizona, New Mexico, and Texas, often found in desert washes and rocky areas. Javelina are classified as herbivores. They eat a variety of native plants and roots. They live in groups, which helps them with survival. Baby javelinas are called reds, because when they are young their hair is a red color. They are not part of the pig family. They belong to a separate family of mammals called the collared peccary.

Wild hogs are known as feral pigs or wild boars and are present in numerous parts of the U.S. They are an invasive species found primarily in the southern third of the United States but are expanding to many other areas. Feral hogs are known for their high reproductive rates and their tendency to root up the ground, which can lead to habitat destruction. They are highly intelligent, social animals with a keen sense of smell and a surprisingly good memory. Wild pigs can be found in various habitats, including deserts, forests, grasslands, and agricultural areas.

There are several types of antelopes, this one is known as the pronghorn. Antelopes have extremely developed senses which help them detect danger. They are quick runners and can run up to 60 mph. They can maintain high speeds for longer periods of time than cheetahs. They like to live in herds. Antelopes don't outrun other animals. They out maneuver them. They can twist and turn very quickly. They are related to cows, sheep, and goats. Both males (bucks) and females (does) have horns, but only males have the distinct, black, forward-pointing prong.

The main difference between a whitetail deer and a Coues whitetail, also known as a desert whitetail or Grey Ghost is size and habitat. Coues whitetails are a smaller subspecies of the white-tailed deer, typically found in the southwestern United States and Mexico, while white-tailed deer are found across a broader range in North America. Coues whitetail Bucks average around 100 pounds and have smaller rack sizes compared to other whitetails.

Burro deer (or burro mule deer) are a specific subspecies of mule deer. They are not a different species, but rather a smaller, lighter-colored desert-dwelling variant of the Rocky Mountain mule deer found in the southwestern US. They are officially known as the Desert Mule Deer or Burro Mule Deer. They are known for having large ears (like a burro or mule), a lighter coat suitable for desert heat, and a white tail with a black tip.

Mule deer get their name because of their mulelike ears. Male deer are called bucks and females are does. Males grow new antlers every year. They can run 45 miles per hour. Mule deer can jump 6 feet high and up to 15 feet in distance. They are bigger than whitetail deer and prefer living in the mountain areas. A mule deer's eyes are located on the side of its head, providing 310 degrees of vision. Mule deer have great night vision.

The bighorn sheep is part of the sheep family and likes to live in desert mountainous areas. Females are called ewes and males are called rams. They are called rams because they like to use their horns to slam into things. Their horn size is a symbol of how high they rank in the herd. The bigger their horns are, the higher they rank. Their large, curled horns can weigh up to 30 pounds. Bighorn sheep are excellent climbers and can stand on ledges as narrow as 2 inches.

Nilgai are large Asian antelopes introduced to South Texas in the 1920s-30s, now boasting a free-ranging population exceeding 38,000. Known as blue bulls, males are large, weighing 400–600+ pounds, with a dark blue-grey coat. Females are smaller, tawny brown, and usually hornless, while males have small, conical horns. They thrive in semi-arid, open scrub country, similar to the Texas brush country. They are mixed feeders, grazing on grass and browsing on trees and shrubs.

Desert burros, or wild donkeys, are highly resilient, intelligent, and social animals that thrive in arid North American environments. They consume a variety of desert vegetation, including grasses, shrubs, and woody plants like mesquite. Burros can lose up to 30% of their body weight in water and replenish it in just five minutes. They can go roughly five days without water. When they can't find water, they dig wells, which helps to provide water for other wildlife.

American desert horses, or mustangs, are feral descendants of Spanish horses brought to the US in the 16th century. Mustangs are known for their extreme endurance, strong legs, and hard hooves, which allow them to thrive in deserts and mountainous regions. They can survive on scarce water, sometimes traveling up to 15 miles a day for water. Wild horses live in small social groups called harems, led by a dominant male, along with several mares (females) and their offspring.

The North American Bison and Buffalo are sometimes confused as the same animal, but they are not. Bison have long hair on their backs, front, and a long beard. Bison are bigger than buffalo. They are the largest mammal in North America and weigh up to 2,000 pounds. Bison can run up to 35 miles per hour. They can jump 6 feet vertically and more than 7 feet horizontally. Bison calves are nicknamed red dogs, because of their orange-red color at birth.

Author Page

Billy Grinslott - Kinsey Marie Books

Copyright, All Rights Reserved

ISBN – 9781968228729

Thanks

www.ingramcontent.com/pod-product-compliance
Lightning Source LLC
Chambersburg PA
CBHW040147240726
48664CB00002B/622